Developing Employees

Pocket Mentor Series

The *Pocket Mentor* Series offers immediate solutions to common challenges managers face on the job every day. Each book in the series is packed with handy tools, self-tests, and real-life examples to help you identify your strengths and weaknesses and hone critical skills. Whether you're at your desk, in a meeting, or on the road, these portable guides enable you to tackle the daily demands of your work with greater speed, savvy, and effectiveness.

Books in the series:

Developing Employees

Expert Solutions
to Everyday Challenges

Harvard Business Press

Boston, Massachusetts

Copyright 2009 Harvard Business School Publishing
All rights reserved
Printed in the United States of America
13 12 11 10 09 5 4 3 2 1

Library of Congress Cataloging-in-Publication Data
Developing employees : expert solutions to everyday challenges.
        p. cm. — (Pocket mentor series)
    ISBN 978-1-4221-2885-5 (pbk. : alk. paper)
   1.   Personnel management. 2.   Career development 3.   Employees—Training of.
 I. Harvard Business School. Press.
    HF5549.D4566 2009
    658.3'124—dc22   2009006659

The paper used in this publication meets the requirements of the American National
Standard for Permanence of Paper for Publications and Documents in Libraries and
Archives Z39.48-1992.

Contents

Tips and Tools

Mentor's Message: Why Develop Your Employees?

Take a moment to think about all the people who report to you. Imagine that each and every one of them could be working to his or her full potential—constantly growing and building new skills, and regularly contributing important value to your team and the entire organization. It's an inspiring vision, isn't it? You can make that vision real by developing your employees.

Employee development is a process aimed at helping your direct reports grow professionally so that they deliver ever greater value to your organization. A manager who excels at developing his or her employees is thus a valuable resource for the company.

In this guide, you'll find a wealth of advice for developing your employees—including how to identify differences among direct reports in terms of their performance and potential, how to adapt your development strategies for each person's unique capacities and needs, and how to conduct development discussions with direct reports.

Developing your employees takes time and energy. But the payoff—a high-performing, loyal team—is well worth it.

Susan Alvey, Mentor

Susan Alvey is an executive coach and leadership development specialist. She also teaches in Babson College's MBA program. From 2001 to 2006, Susan led the learning and organizational development efforts for Harvard Business Publishing. She has served as a facilitator of change and strategic thinking throughout her client organizations. She works closely with corporate executives to ensure that their talent management strategies support their business strategies and that their organizations' structures, roles, and performance measures are aligned to optimize results.

Developing Your Employees: The Basics

The Business Case for Employee Development

A sk three people in your organization to define "employee development," and you will probably receive three different responses. For example:

- **A direct report** may focus on upward mobility ("What can I do to get a promotion?").

- **A manager** may speak to employees' motivation, productivity, and engagement ("What can I do to encourage my employees to do their best work?").

- **A senior-level executive** may address issues such as what it takes to retain and grow top talent to help lead the company in the future ("What do we need to do to ensure that we have the people with the best skills in the right places throughout our company in the future?").

Regardless of your vantage point in the organization, *employee development* can be defined as a process intended to manage employees' professional growth. Ideally, this process is integrated with an organization's performance management program, but it remains distinct from routine performance evaluations.

How your organization benefits

Developing your employees is critical to your organization's success. In fact, as noted in Marcus Buckingham and Curt Coffman's book *First, Break All the Rules* (which discussed a study on employee engagement conducted by the Gallup Organization), research has shown that companies whose employees are inspired to fulfill their greatest potential yield the best business results overall—including profitability, market share, innovation, and efficiency.

Employees who are delivering their best on the job have the energy necessary to generate fresh solutions to organizational problems. They also collaborate better to create innovative products, services, and processes. Moreover, inspired employees generally take pride in their work and feel accountable for their unit's or organization's well-being. Because they are stimulated by their work environment, they also tend to be loyal to the organization.

Your company's plan for developing employees is a key factor in how successfully the enterprise attracts and retains the best talent—those individuals who are best equipped to add to your firm's bottom line. If high-performing individuals feel that they are regularly being given opportunities to grow, they will be more likely to stay with the company, even during tough times. This saves your firm a bundle on recruitment and training costs.

Likewise, having a strong career-development program in place helps your organization prepare for the future. How? It helps you determine who will be in place to take on what assignments in your department or team in the coming years. That way, your employees will stand ready to move into key roles as the need arises. With this sort of succession planning, you help position your organization to respond to new challenges as well as seize new opportunities in the marketplace.

TABLE 1

Two Approaches to Development

Old Approach	New Approach
Only poor performers need development.	Everyone in an organization can be developed, especially high and solid performers.
Development is the responsibility of the human resource group.	Employee development is every manager's responsibility.
Career development focuses on moving capable employees up a predictable corporate ladder.	Career development focuses on moving employees through new challenges to strengthen their professional abilities.
Development means "training" (i.e., internal seminars or weekend workshops).	Development may include training but it also means informal, on-the-job ways of learning, such as <ul><li>"Stretch" assignments</li><li>Job rotations</li><li>Self-paced e-learning</li><li>Action learning</li><li>Manager coaching and feedback</li><li>Mentoring</li></ul>

Comparing old and new approaches to development

Over the past few decades, the approach to employee development has shifted in many organizations. Numerous companies have adopted more expansive models of what development looks like. Table 1 gives you an idea of how these expansive models compare to previous models.

To develop your employees effectively, you must have certain skills, such as the ability to seek out opportunities to unleash direct reports' potential, set development goals for them, and provide feedback they can use to strengthen their talents even further. Equally important, however, you need to feel a deep commitment to cultivating your employees' potential.

As you strive to develop your employees, keep in mind that there is no one-size-fits-all approach. You must respond to your organization's unique business context and to your individual employees' values, skills, and interests. Later in this book, we'll go into more detail about how you can customize your development strategies to each employee's performance, potential, and interests.

You have to water the flowers you want to grow.

—Stephen R. Covey

Your Role

Although an organization's employee development program usually originates in the human resource department, the success of the program hinges on how well managers throughout the company execute the program. Unfortunately, many managers fail to adequately address their employees' developmental needs. Let's look at why this happens and what negative consequences arise from it, and then explore ideas for how you can avoid this all-too-common mistake.

Why some managers neglect employee development

Managers often feel that they don't have the time to invest in developing their direct reports. In light of their busy schedules, they believe that as long as their employees are meeting basic performance expectations, it's enough to address any performance issues during annual or quarterly reviews. And unless an employee actively seeks his or her manager out to talk about professional development, the manager often won't take the time to provide developmental resources such as ideas for mastering new skills or challenges.

Additionally, managers often avoid employee development discussions because these conversations are frequently difficult—for a variety of reasons. To illustrate, Joe, a manager, feels uncomfortable talking to his poor performers because he hasn't yet figured out a clear plan of action for addressing the problem performance. Siobhan, another manager, knows that there are no challenging and interesting new opportunities currently available in her group, so she avoids talking about career development with her high performers because she doesn't want to lose them.

What happens if you neglect it

Although discussing professional development with your employees can be difficult, failing to hold these conversations can adversely affect your unit's performance as well as that of your entire company. How? Your top performers, as well as competent performers, may feel neglected and unmotivated. If these direct reports are not regularly given opportunities to grow or feel supported, their morale and motivation may begin to decline. As a result, they may view their work as less of a priority, and their work habits may deteriorate. They may even defect to a competitor. After all, if top performers don't see any prospects for career growth (these may exist, but might not be immediately apparent), they may seek challenges outside your team—or your organization.

At the other extreme, if you focus on development instead of performance improvement with underachievers, they may wrongly assume that they are doing a good job. These employees might then become disappointed when they don't receive promotions. If they don't know why they haven't been promoted, low performers may share their frustrations with others and spread resentment.

Similarly, there are serious consequences for you as a manager if you ignore employee development. Specifically, you

- Miss the opportunity to align your employees' development with your organization's direction.

- May have unproductive, unhappy employees working for you who poison morale and erode other employees' productivity.

- Don't have backup or "bench strength" among your ranks should a top performer leave.

What Would YOU Do?

Blinded by the Stars?

JACK STARTED AS DIRECTOR OF RESEARCH at Rose, Greene, & Bloom LLC, a statistical analysis firm, one year ago. He prided himself on his ability to grow his star employees, and was confident that he had addressed performance issues with his underachievers to the best of his ability.

But one morning, he overheard some troubling news. One of his most reliable and competent employees, Ana, had started to look for a new job because she felt ignored and underappreciated. Jack was surprised; Ana seemed so content. In fact, she'd never needed much of his attention. Jack was eager to take immediate action to retain Ana, but wasn't sure where to start.

What would YOU do? The mentor will suggest a solution in *What You COULD Do.*

Not surprisingly, all this can reflect badly on you and damage your own prospects in the organization.

What I need is someone who will make me do what I can.
—Ralph Waldo Emerson

How you can fulfill this role

Effective employee development depends on your ability to match your employees' growth opportunities with your company's needs. However, although you are responsible for guiding your direct reports' development, your employees themselves need to feel a sense of ownership over the process of managing their careers. As we'll see, you can help them acquire this sense of ownership by involving them in regular discussions about their career opportunities in the organization.

As a manager, you share ownership of the employee development process as well. Your role consists of the following set of activities:

- Helping your employees to match their skills, business interests, and work values with job opportunities

- Conducting frequent discussions of your direct reports' developmental needs

- Giving timely and specific feedback about an individual's performance against the expectations you've established together

What You COULD Do

Remember Jack's concern about how to keep Ana with the company?

Here's what the mentor suggests:

Like many managers, Jack made the mistake of concentrating all of his effort and time on developing top employees and managing the performance of underachievers. As a result, he neglected the people in the middle—the B players, the solid contributors who consistently meet expectations but are not standouts. Ana is one of them.

To retain Ana, Jack needs to first recognize her contribution and communicate her value. He should check with her to determine the direction she'd like her career to take, but should be careful not to impose his own desire for advancement on her. If Ana would like to take on new career responsibilities, Jack should take an inventory of her skills, interests, and values. He should then seek out development opportunities to match them. When he feels prepared to discuss the available opportunities, he should meet with Ana to create a development plan agreeable to both of them.

- Providing coaching when necessary to help employees reach agreed-upon goals

- Acting as an informal teacher by being aware of the behaviors and attitudes you're modeling (for example, taking initiative for your own career development)

- Working with your employees to draft individual development plans

Customizing Development Strategies for Employees

As a manager, you probably know that no two employees have exactly the same developmental needs. However, you may not know the critical role that differentiating between employees—in terms of their performance and potential—plays in the success of your organization. Below, we examine this topic and explore strategies for differentiating employees.

The importance of seeing employees' differences

Employees are different in terms of their developmental needs. When you identify these differences, you generate important results for your organization. Specifically, you

- **Appropriately address performance expectations.** What is a realistic expectation of performance for one employee may not be for another, even if they share the same job title. For example, a person who has just started out in a role will probably need different types of development opportunities than someone who has worked in that same job for a longer stretch of time.

- **Draft suitable developmental plans.** Whereas some employees may need only stretch goals to provide them with on-the-job challenges, others may need goals directed at improving their performance. When you distinguish between these two needs, you can more easily create the right developmental plans for each direct report.

- **Help direct reports manage their careers.** Tailoring a development program to the specific needs of individual employees improves their chances of succeeding in their current *and* future jobs. Successful direct reports not only help produce valuable business results for your company but also tend to be more loyal to the firm. The more loyal, high-performing employees your company has, the less it has to spend on recruiting and training new hires and dealing with the disruption that comes with high turnover of staff members.

- **Build a stronger foundation for your organization's success.** When you know who your top performers are, you can help your organization focus its retention efforts on these individuals so rival organizations don't steal them away.

Ways of differentiating employees

What does *differentiation* mean, exactly? Simply stated, it is the process by which managers assess their team members to provide them with appropriate growth and job-enrichment opportunities. What criteria should you use to assess your employees during this process? Many organizations differentiate employees according to performance. Using this model, managers divide their direct reports into three groups:

- **Top performers:** These are employees who define the standard for exceptional performance by consistently delivering exemplary results and motivating others to do so as well.

- **Solid performers:** These are employees who consistently meet expectations but may not be on a fast track within the organization.

- **Underperformers:** These are employees who just get by, delivering barely acceptable results.

Other firms choose to designate their employees' performance in more relative terms. For example, in a given group or unit, top performers would be the best 10 percent to 20 percent; solid performers, the middle 60 percent to 80 percent; and underperformers, the bottom 10 percent to 20 percent. However, such forced ranking systems have generated controversy in many organizations. Opponents of such systems maintain that because only a few people can be ranked as top performers, forced ranking may foster an intimidating, competitive environment. In addition, many managers find it difficult to assign a certain percentage of their employees—especially if they are performing adequately—to the lowest rank.

Treat people as if they were what they ought to be and you help them to become what they are capable of being.
—Goethe

An alternative way to assess employees' differences is to factor in each employee's potential as well as current performance. By considering potential, you take into account not only the employee's historical contribution but also his or her future value to your firm. With that in mind, let's now consider a tool that helps you factor in both the current performance and future potential of each employee.

Using the Performance and Potential Grid

As we've seen, there are a number of ways to evaluate your employees' developmental needs. Your company's human resource group may recommend specific tools, so it's best to start by checking in with that group. If your organization does not recommend a preferred tool, consider using the following Performance and Potential Grid, a powerful tool we discuss in detail below.

Introducing the grid

As the name suggests, the Performance and Potential Grid helps you place an employee on a matrix in terms of his or her current performance and future potential value to the firm. Each of the nine cells in the matrix maps to a specific category and set of recommended actions (see figure 1).

FIGURE 1

The Performance and Potential Grid

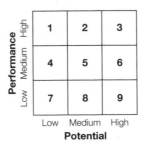

For example, you would place an employee with medium performance and high potential in cell 6—and follow a specific course of action to develop that person.

The worksheet for using the Performance and Potential Grid (located in the Tools section for this topic) provides a series of questions to help you identify your employees' performance and potential levels, along with a list of corresponding action steps.

Evaluating an employee's performance

To use the Performance and Potential Grid, first establish an individual's performance level. You can arrive at this level by answering six yes-or-no questions about your direct report's performance. These questions are shown in table 2.

TABLE 2

Assessing an Employee's Performance

To assess an employee's performance, ask yourself the following questions:

1. Does this employee *exceed* expectations in at least one area of performance?

2. Does this employee exceed expectations in *most* (or *all*) areas of performance?

3. Does this employee meet or exceed expectations in *all* areas of performance?

4. Is the employee a key contributor to the team and the organization?

5. Does the employee act on corrective performance feedback in order to improve performance?

6. Have you provided significant, specific performance rewards to this employee (special bonus, formal recognition, etc.)?

Assign the employee one point for each question to which you answered "yes." To determine the employee's performance level, add up the total number of points. A total of 0 to 2 points indicates low performance. A total of 3 to 4 points suggests medium performance. A total of 5 to 6 points means high performance.

For example, Javier, a manager, answers the six questions for his direct report Isabel. He tallies the results and arrives at a total score of 3 (three "yes" responses in total). According to this system, Isabel is a medium performer.

Evaluating an employee's potential

Now that you've evaluated your employee's current performance, you'll want to determine his or her potential. You'll determine this by answering ten yes-or-no questions, shown in table 3.

Again, for each question you answer in the affirmative, give the employee one point. If you are unsure about how to answer a particular question, it's better to give the person the higher score by responding "yes." The employee's potential level is determined by adding up the total number of points: 0 to 3 points indicates low potential, 4 to 7 points means medium potential, and 8 to 10 points suggests high potential.

Let's look again at the example of Javier and Isabel. Javier answers the ten questions about Isabel's potential. He tallies the results and comes up with a total of five "yes" responses. He thus assigns her 5 points for her potential. Therefore, using this system, Isabel has medium potential.

TABLE 3

Assessing an Employee's Potential

To assess an employee's potential, ask yourself the following questions:

1. Could the employee perform at a higher level, in a different position, or take on increased responsibilities within the next *one* year? (Consider the person's ability only, not whether there is a position available to support this growth.)

2. Could the employee perform at a higher level, in a different position, or take on increased responsibilities within the next *three* years? (Consider the person's ability only, not whether there is a position available to support this growth.)

3. Can you envision this employee performing two levels above his or her current position in the next five to six years?

4. Is the organization likely to value growth of the skills and competencies of this employee over the next several years?

5. Could the employee learn the additional skills and competencies he or she needs to be able to perform at a higher or different level?

6. Does the employee demonstrate leadership ability—for example, by showing initiative and vision, delivering on promised results, communicating effectively, and taking appropriate risks?

7. Does the employee demonstrate an ability to comfortably interact with people at a higher level or in different areas?

8. Does the employee demonstrate comfort with a broader company perspective than his or her job currently requires?

9. Does the employee demonstrate flexibility and motivation to move into a job that might be different than any that currently exists?

10. Does the employee welcome opportunities for learning and development?

What Would YOU Do?

Jilted at the Phones

L UKE WAS RECENTLY RECRUITED to head up the customer service group at Robbco Manufacturing. After three months, Luke is comfortable with his three direct reports, Cecilia, Peter, and Jill, and feels he knows their strengths and weaknesses on the job. He recognizes that one of his key responsibilities as a manager is to develop his employees, and he's ready to make this a priority.

During informal conversations with each of his employees to discuss their business interests, Luke learns that his top employee, Cecilia, would like to get more involved in developing corporate policy. Luke speaks with his colleague in human resources, Marina, and informs her of Cecilia's interests. It turns out that Marina is leading a cross-functional task force on company morale that's convening on Thursday—and she thinks Cecilia would be a good addition to the team.

Luke is excited about this opportunity and schedules a career development discussion with Cecilia for the next morning at 9:00. When he arrives in the office at 8:30 the morning of the meeting, he's surprised to find that Jill has not yet arrived; she was assigned to cover the phones for the rest of the team starting at 8:30. Annoyed, Luke covers the phones himself until Jill finally arrives at 9:00. He's concerned. According to his documentation,

Jill has missed early call duty three times since he's come on board.

He wonders how best to juggle this developmental need with his other employees' needs. Should he postpone his meeting with Cecilia to promptly address Jill's performance issues? Schedule a meeting with Jill later in the week to discuss the problem? Give Jill the benefit of the doubt and see whether she continues to come in late?

What would YOU do? The mentor will suggest a solution in *What You COULD Do*.

Placing the employee on the grid

Now that you've evaluated your employee's performance and potential, it's time to place him or her on the Performance and Potential Grid. How should you do this? You plot the intersection of the low, medium, or high designations for both performance and potential. The intersection will place the employee in a cell from 1 to 9. These cells map to the following categories:

- Cell 2, 3, or 6 = top employee

- Cell 1, 4, or 5 = solid contributor

- Cell 7, 8, or 9 = underperformer

To return to the example: because Isabel's performance level is medium and her potential is medium, Javier would place her in cell 5 (figure 2). According to the categories listed above, he would thus characterize her as a solid contributor.

FIGURE 2

Placing Your Employees on the Grid

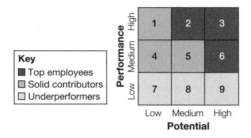

Key
■ Top employees
▣ Solid contributors
☐ Underperformers

Using the grid to determine next steps

Once you've placed an employee on the Performance and Potential Grid, your next step is to determine the best course of action for him or her. Returning to our example, Javier has determined that Isabel is a solid contributor. That means she's both valuable and productive. The suggested course of action for developing solid contributors includes keeping them engaged and motivated through recognition, as well as focusing on improving their performance. With solid contributors, you might also test to see whether they're capable of greater accomplishment. If so, you can provide appropriate developmental opportunities. You'll also want to keep watch for increases in a solid contributor's performance and potential.

More broadly speaking, you'll want to consider the following guidelines after you've determined each employee's level.

- Be sure to invest in your top employees (your 2s, 3s, and 6s).
  What resources do you have to invest in these people to keep

What You COULD Do

Remember Luke's worries about how to deal with Jill and Cecilia?

Here's what the mentor suggests:

Luke should meet with Cecilia as planned and schedule a meeting with Jill later in the week to discuss her performance issues. Yes, he needs to meet with Jill in a timely fashion—but this could wait a few days. Waiting to meet with Jill would not only give Luke more time to prepare, it would also acknowledge his commitment to developing his top employee, Cecilia. Luke would be wise to concentrate his time and efforts on developing his A players—those who are the most productive and contribute the most to the company. Taking such an action maximizes the return on his time and energy as a manager. When Luke does meet with Jill, an underperformer, he should make it clear that the meeting is about addressing her performance issues, not about career development.

them appropriately challenged? What motivation can you provide to keep them satisfied? Be aware that there may not be much room for advancement for top employees within your group. Think about alternative ways to engage them and help them grow professionally.

- **Strive to affirm and grow your solid contributors (your 1s, 4s, and 5s).** What can you do to ensure that they stay satisfied and productive? Consider whether there are opportunities for growth for them within your team and organization.

- **Act decisively with underperforming team members who lack initiative (your 7s, 8s, and 9s).** Identify the people on your team who lack initiative and continually underperform. What might you do to ensure that their inadequate performance is dealt with or that they are in a job that best suits them? How should you determine whether a dismissal is in order?

The next three sections go into detail about each of these guidelines in turn.

Keeping Top Employees Motivated

Satisfying the needs of your star performers and nurturing their professional growth is critical to your organization's success. Your best employees, the A players, boost the company performance, both directly (by working diligently at their jobs) and indirectly (by inspiring and motivating others around them). Therefore, it's critical that you invest the time and energy to keep them satisfied and engaged. Below, we explore ideas for doing so.

Comparing extrinsic versus intrinsic motivators

In the past, managers often focused their motivation efforts on what are commonly known as extrinsic factors—those aspects of a job that are related to job *environment*, not the content of the job itself. These extrinsic motivators included

- Company policies and benefits

- Working conditions

- Salary and other forms of compensation

- Status

Today, successful managers understand that externally focused incentives often provide only short-term motivation. They understand that appealing to people's inner drives, needs, and desires can achieve better results. This type of motivation relies on so-called intrinsic factors that are related to *job content*. And it arises from within employees. Intrinsic motivators include

- On-the-job-achievement

- Positive feedback about the quality of the person's work

- Opportunities for growth and learning

- A sense of responsibility for the work being done

Identifying what motivates your best employees

Finding out what motivates each of your top employees is critical. The easiest way to do this is simply to ask these A players directly. Set up frank conversations to find out what they would like to be doing and what drives them to do their best. Ask them questions such as the following:

- What kinds of work are you most passionate about?

- What types of opportunities for learning do you find most exciting?

- What types of rewards most motivate you? Are you most energized by money, autonomy, the chance to work with people you like or admire, job title, time off, intellectual challenge?

Sometimes these questions can be difficult for people to answer. You may have to deduce the answers by asking less direct questions, such as: What do you like, or not like, about your job? Alternatively, you may simply pay attention to your employees' behavior, taking note of the tasks they seem to enjoy and what seems to motivate them the most.

Also, be sure to find out whether anything about their job situation is frustrating them, such as too much travel, difficult colleagues, or not enough challenge from day to day. Try to address their needs and desires—and eliminate obstacles as best you can. Help them to develop by shaping their careers and responsibilities in the direction they'd like to go. To move them in the right direction, you'll have to provide them with the right growth opportunities.

It is time for us to stand and cheer for the doer, the achiever, the one who recognizes the challenge and does something about it.

—Vince Lombardi

Providing appropriate challenges

Providing the A players on your team with appropriate challenges does not necessarily require promoting them. It may be enough to simply expand or redefine a star performer's current role to keep him or her stimulated and engaged. The key is to have your best employees perform tasks that they do not already know how to do—or that they don't yet do well. You can keep these individuals engaged and growing by increasing their responsibilities and stretching the boundaries of their current jobs. Many experts refer to this as *job enrichment*.

Ideally, you will be able to match your star performers with assignments that both interest and challenge them—and that benefit the organization. Keep in mind that job-enrichment opportunities often exist outside the boundaries of your unit or group. As a manager, you are in a better position to seek these opportunities out. Work with human resources or within your own organizational network to identify special assignments, teams, or other opportunities within the company that A players may find intriguing.

Ability is of little account without opportunity.
  —Napoleon Bonaparte

Consider the following learning experiences:

- **Ask your top performers to start new projects from scratch.** For example, invite an A player to develop and launch a new product or head up a new initiative or task force.

- **Give high-potential employees the opportunities to fix businesses or products in trouble.** For example, task one of them with improving the bottom line of a new service, or invite him or her to try marketing a struggling product to a new customer segment.

- **Provide A players with job rotations in different work environments.** For example, assign a marketing manager to do a stint in the sales organization, or a logistics person to work in the international group for a while.

- **Assign your best performers high-profile special projects.** These projects, which should have very clear objectives and a short duration, offer talented employees the chance to practice targeted problem solving, work in cross-functional teams, and gain that all-important exposure to senior executives. Project-based assignments like these also offer the added benefit of flexibility. Often, participants can work on such projects part-time, so they would not have to give up their current duties.

You should be prepared to provide your A players with adequate support to meet these challenges, whether that support takes the form of active coaching, mentoring, or a systematic review-and-feedback process. Don't just throw the assignment at them and see whether they sink or swim.

Steps for Identifying Career Development Opportunities for Your Employees

1. **Consider the performance and potential of the employee.** Start by differentiating your employees based on performance and potential. You'll want to focus your energy on helping the top and solid performers develop and grow. If an employee is underperforming, you'll want to address performance issues— not development plans—at this point.

2. **Review the employee's interests and values.** Consider both the work and personal interests you identified in your preliminary conversations and development discussions. For example, does the employee enjoy fieldwork? Does he or she prioritize a work/life balance over other interests? Also consider what motivates the employee. Does he or she value change and

variety? Is he or she interested in learning about new business units?

3. **Make a list of opportunities that match the employee's interests, skills, and potential.** Opportunities can take the form of promotions, new work assignments, lateral transfers, special projects or initiatives, or temporary assignments. They can also include trying a new role on a project, such as leading a conference call or making a presentation to a client.

4. **Get input from people outside your group or business unit.** To find out whether opportunities outside of your group or business unit exist, consult individuals in the human resource department and colleagues in other groups. Ask them for ideas for possible assignments for this employee. Make sure to indicate the types of challenges you think are appropriate based on this employee's skills, interests, and values.

5. **Present your ideas to the employee.** Your role as a manager is to guide the employee by helping to match his or her skills, interests, and values with opportunities. You'll want to suggest both short-term opportunities and longer-term prospects. However, don't make any promises about long-term options. Instead, focus on immediate options for the employee and suggest what other possibilities might be available in the future.

Providing mentors for top talent

Some organizations have established mentoring programs for high-potential employees. These programs pair individuals with experts who are willing to guide them in meeting certain work

Tips for Helping Top Performers Find Mentors

- Look for individuals who are able to understand and shape the employee's long-term professional goals (e.g., someone who has a similar background or who is currently in a position the employee might like to have in the future).
- Consider people who are influential within the company. These individuals know how the organization works and can help your employee navigate the system.
- Think about someone who possesses a higher level of functional experience than the employee. Sometimes individuals outside your company or outside the chain of command, such as someone in a trade organization, are the best mentors.
- Look for someone with a skill set that is broader than the employee's. Although you want the individuals to connect with each other, you also want the relationship to help your employee grow and develop in new ways.
- Defining how the relationship should work can help both the mentor and your direct report. For example, how often should they meet? What types of things should they discuss? What are the rules for confidentiality?
- Ask your employee what he or she wants to get from a mentoring relationship to help you find the right fit.

Additional Tips for Managing Your Top Talent

To further manage your best performers:

- **Foster collaboration among talented people in your organization.** People often stay in organizations because they enjoy the company of like-minded colleagues, so make an effort to bring your best employees together with other talented people in the company. You can do this informally by creating social networking opportunities, or more formally by finding opportunities for your star players to take part in special task forces or work groups.

- **Look for signs of burnout.** Highly motivated employees are often prone to overwork. Examine your actions: Is it possible that you are overloading your star performers? If so, correct this behavior quickly, or you'll risk losing your best employees to exhaustion.

challenges and in defining a satisfying career path that also benefits the company. If your organization doesn't have such a program, consider establishing an informal one for your top employees.

Finding appropriate mentors for your best performers need not be an arduous task. Mentors do not necessarily even have to be a part of your group or business unit. In fact, mentors outside the organization may be able to offer broader perspectives and thus provide even better support for your star players.

For the high-potential individual, having a mentor can be critical. Mentors know how to motivate employees by providing recognition for specific achievements. Beyond just offering encouragement, however, mentors can help top-performing employees

- Clarify their career options

- Better understand and navigate the organization's politics

- Build support networks with people inside and outside the company

- Deal with work obstacles such as resource shortages, uncooperative colleagues, or confusing priorities

Skilled mentors help employees do their jobs better. In a recent survey of individuals who stated that they had a good mentoring experience, 97 percent of the respondents said that the experience contributed directly to their success at the company.

Growing Competent Employees

I t's easy to recognize the employees in your organization who bring in the biggest revenues or win awards. But there are others who are also important: those competent employees, or B players, who consistently meet expectations even if they are not standout performers. Although these people may not seek the limelight, it's still critical for managers to recognize, value, and develop them. Let's look at how you might do this.

Understanding and appreciating your "corporate backbone"

Steady, reliable performers are your corporate backbone; they keep your organization going, day by day. These employees are valuable to your organization because they often

- **Have a deep understanding of an organization's history and processes.** They have strong institutional memory of what has worked in the past and what hasn't—whether it's a particular type of change initiative, a business process, or a way of managing a product or service. They are frequently comfortable in their jobs and are likely to want to stay in them.

- **Adapt to large-scale organizational change more easily than many A players because they feel less threatened by it.** Your solid contributors can help other people through the trauma of change by providing focus and reassurance.

- Were former superstars who left the fast track for a variety of reasons, such as the desire to improve the balance between work and their personal life. Therefore, they may have the skills needed to take on more responsibility during crises.

To retain your solid contributors, you'll need to develop them in ways that best match their competencies, potential, and desires.

Developing these solid contributors

To develop your solid contributors, begin the same way you would with your star performers: seek to understand their most passionate business interests, deepest work values, and strongest skills. Find out what direction they'd like their career to take.

Don't be surprised if members of this group are not eager—or able—to advance in the organization. Instead of pushing them, allow them the freedom to stay where they are. Periodically check in with them to find out whether they are interested in career advancement. You might also "test" individuals in this group to determine whether they're capable of greater accomplishment. For instance, by giving them the right developmental opportunities and encouragement, you may discover that some of your competent players are capable of becoming stars.

Identify solid-performing employees who have growth potential and provide them with "stretch" assignments. The best assignments are those that offer them challenges that encourage them to learn new skills and acquire new knowledge. Match employees to these assignments carefully to ensure that they are not overwhelmed.

Some solid contributors may also benefit from coaching. By entering into coaching partnerships, you share your knowledge and experience as a manager to help maximize employees' potential and assist them in achieving agreed-upon goals. This ongoing, two-way process relies on collaboration and requires a positive emotional bond between coach and protégé.

Also consider encouraging motivated and competent employees to enhance specific job or life skills through training. This can take many forms, including sessions provided by internal human resources staff, seminars delivered by experts in a particular field, college or university courses, and online or distance-learning classes.

Your B players are also good candidates for lateral movements. Giving these employees new experiences through job rotations or "sideways promotions" can help keep them energized and productive.

Providing frequent affirmation

Make a deliberate effort to let these "supporting actors" of the corporate world know that they are important and that you and the rest of the organization value their contributions. Without some level of affirmation, they may lose their motivation and their enthusiasm for the job. For example:

- **Tell them that they are valued.** Show that you have a genuine interest in them by letting them know how important they are to you, your team, and the organization overall.

- **Listen to their ideas.** When they offer a suggestion, listen carefully. Take the time to respond thoughtfully and respectfully. If you act on a suggestion, be sure to give them credit.

- **Praise their accomplishments.** Be conscious of the aspects of their jobs at which they are particularly good. Tell them—and others—how much you appreciate their unique talents.

- **Trust them.** Show them that you have confidence in them by allowing them to take actions and make decisions that are appropriate for their skill level.

Tips for Nurturing Solid Contributors

- Keep track of communications with your employees to make sure that you are not ignoring solid contributors.
- Tell these employees on a regular basis that they are valued.
- Be creative with your rewards, both large and small. Don't be afraid to send an e-mail, leave a voicemail, or give the employee a special bonus to acknowledge his or her contributions.
- Accept that some people in your group will not want to advance further in their careers. Don't push them. Instead, look for ways to keep their jobs interesting, without burdening them with unwanted new responsibilities.
- Allocate resources to solid performers with high potential. Consider providing a mentor, coaching, interesting learning opportunities, or a combination of these.

Above all, accept your competent employees for who they are: solid performers on whom your team and organization rely. Make a point of discovering who among them has the motivation and capability to grow into positions with greater responsibility. Groom these people as you would A players—by giving them developmental resources and opportunities. But also respect those B players who are content where they are.

Dealing with Underperformers

As you may have gathered by now, developing your employees can be time-intensive. Matching your direct reports' interests, values, and skills to growth opportunities based on their level of performance and potential requires careful consideration. Therefore, you should invest your employee development time and energy carefully. That means focusing your development efforts on your topmost performers and your competent employees as well as dealing effectively with your underperformers—those C players who aren't delivering the results your team and organization need.

Calculating the return-on-management ratio

To understand this point about investing your employee development time and energy carefully, you may find it helpful to first consider something known as the return-on-management (ROM) ratio of developing your direct reports, proposed by Robert Simons and Antonio Davila in their April 2005 *Harvard Business Review* article "How High Is Your Return on Management?" The ROM ratio can be expressed as follows:

$$\text{ROM} = \frac{\text{Productive energy released}}{\text{Management time and attention invested}}$$

This ratio—which is more of a metaphor than an exact calculation—provides a framework for evaluating how you invest your time and energy during your day-to-day work. Is your energy invested in activities that best contribute to your organization's productivity and overall performance? If not, you are probably not spending your time on the right opportunities and challenges.

When it comes to developing employees, the ROM ratio suggests that managers should spend most of their time and energy working with the people who contribute the most and add the most value to the organization. This group would consist of both star performers and solid contributors. Based on such an assessment, the third group, your low-potential, low-performing employees (or C players) would merit the least management time and energy because they benefit the organization the least.

Identifying C players

Although the ROM ratio indicates that those who deliver mediocre performance and lack initiative deserve the least attention, you obviously cannot simply ignore them. Instead, you must take the time up front to identify who your C players are and then take decisive action. Failing to deal with your low-performing employees can have a detrimental effect on your unit's and organization's performance. These individuals often

- Stand in the way of the advancement of more talented employees

- Hire other C players, which lowers the performance bar across the board

- Tend to be poor role models who encourage a low-performer mentality among their peers and direct reports

- Engender a culture of mediocrity that repels highly talented and ambitious people away from your team and company

Once you've differentiated these employees, you must decide how you will manage them. Then, it's best to act decisively—but with respect.

Moving underperformers up or out

Generally speaking, the strategy for dealing with any C players in your group centers on addressing their underperformance. The first step is to try to move them up to an acceptable performance level. To do this:

- Provide them with clearly defined expectations for performance.

- Create a prescribed path and timeline for achieving those goals.

- Be explicit about the ways in which they must improve.

- Be willing to coach and provide candid feedback.

Some employees may be unable—or unwilling—to improve their performance, however. The best course of action for these individuals is to move them out of their current jobs. This may mean trying to find them a different position in your organization where they may be more successful, or dismissing them from the company.

Deciding whether dismissal is in order

Before dismissing an employee, you'll want to determine whether this is truly the right step or whether you have any other recourse. If you have exhausted your options, make sure you have thorough and accurate documentation of the employee's performance or behavior problems and the steps you've taken to help him or her improve. Finally, consult with your legal and human resource departments regarding the dismissal regulations unique to your situation.

Dismissing an employee is often a painful process. You may find it helpful to keep in mind your ultimate goal in taking this action: to strengthen your talent pool in order to enhance business performance. Your first allegiance must be to your organization, not to an individual. If C players remain under your supervision, you are compromising your company's performance—and your own career.

Also, remember that letting employees languish in a job where they are not respected by their direct reports and peers only hurts them. Moving them out is not only good for your organization but good for the employees as well.

Discussing Career Development with Your Employees

You've used a Performance and Potential Grid or similar tool to determine who on your team are the top employees and solid contributors—the people you want to develop—and who in your group are underperformers who need to be helped, moved, or dismissed. The next step is to work with your star players and solid contributors to create plans that will help them grow. To create such plans, you'll need to conduct career development discussions with each employee.

Whether you are trying to identify a challenging special project or an appropriate stretch assignment for a particular employee, you'll need to have a series of one-on-one conversations with him or her. Below, we explore ideas for preparing for and conducting such discussions.

Preparing for the discussion

The content of career development conversations will differ depending on the employee in question and his or her performance and potential. However, you will prepare for each of these discussions in the same way. You'll also want to ask each employee to prepare. Help the employee by handing out the "Employees' Planning Worksheet" in the Tools section at the end of the book, which the employee can fill out before your meeting.

Do your own homework, too. Use as many sources as possible to try to assemble the most complete picture of your direct report.

Look for any documentation you might have on file, including the employee's

- Past developmental plans

- Individual self-appraisals, if they exist

- Performance reviews

- History of training or courses attended

Next, you'll want to clarify how ready you are to conduct a career development discussion. You should be able to answer the following questions adequately:

- **What are the employee's skills?** Describe your employee's abilities and the knowledge that he or she has developed. These skills fall into many categories, from leadership and management to analytical abilities and creative innovation.

- **What are the employee's interests and values?** What is most important to this employee in terms of managing his or her work and personal life? What provides meaning in the work this person does? To answer these questions accurately, you may need to ask the person directly, or help him or her use career-assessment instruments.

- **What opportunities are available to the employee?** What tasks or assignments offer challenges that would encourage the employee to build his or her skills and acquire new knowledge? What other job functions might be appropriate given this person's transferable skills?

Steps for Preparing for a Career Development Discussion

1. **Schedule the meeting.** Tell the employee well in advance of the actual meeting that you want to have the discussion. This gives both parties time to prepare. Be sure to pick a time and location that will minimize distractions.

2. **Agree on content.** Clarify the purpose of the meeting: to have an open, honest discussion about the employee's growth and discuss possible opportunity. Ask the employee to prepare for the meeting by thinking about his or her skills, goals, and interests.

3. **Gather information on the employee.** Consult several sources, including the employee's past development plans, individual self-appraisals (if they exist), performance reviews, and training history. Talk informally with the employee and other coworkers about his or her skills, interests, and values.

4. **Reflect on the employee's skills, interests, and values.** Write down the employee's strengths and weakness. Then, write down what you perceive to be the employee's interests and values. Consider whether you think the employee is likely to want more responsibility. Keep in mind that some solid performers are content to stay in their current roles. As you create a list, develop questions you may want to ask the employee to get a better understanding of his or her interests and goals.

5. **Explore the opportunities available to the employee.** Think about what tasks or assignments might offer the employee opportunities to build skills and acquire new knowledge. Talk with other managers, your supervisor, or the human resource department to generate a list of possibilities.

If you can't answer these questions, do more research before having your development conversation. If you haven't spent the time to uncover an employee's skills, interests, and values, or sought the opportunities in your organization to match them, the development discussion may be unproductive and even frustrating for the employee.

Establishing trust

An effective career development discussion requires more than preparation; it also requires having the employee's trust. If you have not secured the person's trust, he or she may question whether you can truly offer honest advice untainted by an agenda.

How can you gain your employee's trust? The following tips can help:

- **Be reliable.** For example, conduct the conversation when you said you would, and arrive on time.

- **Speak authentically.** For instance, express genuine appreciation for the employee's contributions and cite specific examples of how those contributions have helped your team and the organization succeed in the business arena.

- **Listen for understanding.** To illustrate, paraphrase what you're hearing the employee say about his or her career goals to show that you understand correctly what the person has communicated.

- **Keep your commitments.** For example, if during the development conversation you promise to explore specific special assignments for the employee, explain how you intend to keep that promise.

Without trust, employees will likely be guarded during the career development discussion. This leads to a superficial and often ineffective conversation, and that means valuable time wasted.

Conducting the discussion

When you begin the development meeting, reiterate the purpose and importance of the discussion. That is, take some time to help the employee understand that you are genuinely interested in his or her success. Make sure that your direct report understands that he or she is responsible for working with you to create a developmental plan—and for sticking to it. Help the employee understand that career development is forward looking, unlike performance assessment, which is backward looking.

Next, share your perceptions about the employee's skills, interests, and values. For example, have you observed signals that the person would like to develop his or her presentation abilities? That he or she is interested in learning how to lead a team? That the individual would value opportunities to work with more creative people? Verify the accuracy of these assumptions and gather more

Additional Tips for Building Trust

- Be open, honest, and direct in all of your communications. When people see you as sincere and committed, they are more likely to believe that you have their best interests in mind.
- Make it a priority to listen to others' concerns to demonstrate your openness to their ideas. Establish an environment where everyone can share their ideas and know that their opinions are valued.
- Be consistent in demonstrating your concern for your employees' success.
- Share or give credit to those who contribute good ideas.
- Acknowledge your own weaknesses. When you recognize your own flaws, people see you as being a truthful person and will likely trust you more.
- Remember that it takes time to build trust, but trust can be broken quickly.

information by asking pointed questions. Listen actively to the responses and check whether you've heard correctly.

Then talk about the development opportunities you've identified—any special assignments, training programs, job rotations, or other ideas you've come up with that you think would make a good match for your employee. Discuss the options—and limitations—within the person's current job and the organization as a whole as they relate to the employee's skills, interests, and values.

Be realistic and honest, so you don't create false expectations for promotions or other opportunities that may not materialize.

Defining a development plan

Once you've reached agreement on the employee's skills, interests, and values as well as the development opportunities that seem most promising, you and your employee are ready to draft a development plan. The plan should contain the following information:

- **Specific goals,** along with a timeline for achieving them

- **Action steps,** which may include training, coaching, challenging work assignments, and so forth

Because the career development discussion is collaborative, you and your employee will likely need more than one meeting to perfect a development plan. Once the two of you have created a final version of the plan, seek the employee's commitment to achieving the goals, action steps, and timelines set forth in the plan.

Then establish a follow-up schedule to ensure accountability. During follow-up, you'll monitor the person's progress on a regular basis. Scheduling periodic check-ins with the employee will help you determine whether he or she needs additional training, coaching, or support. Likewise, this process will help ensure that you are following through on your own commitment to the development process.

Tips for Creating an Individual Development Plan

- The development plan should be a collaborative effort between you and your direct report. Work with the employee to create achievable goals that he or she can remain enthusiastic about over the long term.
- Aim to make at least 70 percent of the suggested action items on-the-job learning, such as stretch assignments.
- Aim to make less than 20 percent of the suggested development activities training programs or other formal education programs.
- Be sure to include opportunities for coaching the employee.
- Focus your plan on leveraging strengths as well as overcoming weaknesses.
- Include an expected outcome and time frame for each action item to establish accountability and to help ensure that the employee stays on track.
- Make the plan challenging enough to push the employee to the edge of his or her comfort zone in the areas targeted for development.
- Help the employee recruit at least one person who will help hold him or her accountable to the goals described in the development plan.

Tips and Tools

Tools for Developing Your Employees

Employee's Planning Worksheet for Development Discussions

Use the following questions to help you think about your developmental needs and goals before you meet with your manager to discuss them.

Interests and Values

What are your professional interests and values? *For example, what types of projects do you enjoy? Are you motivated by compensation? By increased responsibility?*

What are your lifestyle needs? *For example, limited or no travel, set work schedule, etc.*

Skills: Strengths and Gaps

What are your top five skills (i.e., those where you have the most proficiency and/or those you enjoy using the most)?

What do you believe are the top two or three skills you need to learn in order to grow in your job, advance to the next level, or seek a new job?

What are your key transferable skills—those skills that are not just job-specific but that can be applied to work in many positions? *For example: basic computer skills, negotiation skills, financial analysis.*

Do you think you are currently performing up to your potential? Why or why not?

Job Satisfaction

What is your overall level of satisfaction with your current position? Are you beginning to sense it's time for a change?

What parts of your work would you like to continue doing, or do with more skill?

What new work activities or positions would you like to try?

Career Goals and Next Steps

What would you like to be doing six to twelve months from now?

What do you need to do to get there? *For example: What types of projects would you need to work on? What type of experience would you need to get? What type of training would you need?*

What would you like to be doing three to five years from now?

What do you need to do to get there? *For example: What types of projects would you need to work on? What type of experience would you need to get? What type of training would you need?*

Worksheet for Using the Performance and Potential Grid

Use this tool to assess your employees' performance and potential and to start to develop a plan for their growth.

NAME OF EMPLOYEE:

Part I: Defining Performance		
Question	**Yes**	**No**
1. Does this employee *exceed* expectations in at least one area of performance?		
2. Would you say that this employee exceeds expectations in *most* (or *all*) areas of performance?		
3. Does this employee meet or exceed expectations in *all* areas of performance?		
4. Is the employee a key contributor to the team and the organization?		
5. Does the employee act on corrective performance feedback in order to improve performance?		
6. Have you provided significant, specific performance rewards to this employee (special bonus, formal recognition, etc.)?		
TOTALS		

*To evaluate this employee's **performance**, calculate the total number of "yes" responses and use the following scoring:*
0–1 = Low; 2–4 = Medium; 5–6 = High

Part II: Defining Potential		
Question	**Yes**	**No**
1. Could the employee perform at a higher level, in a different position, or take on increased responsibilities within the next year? (Consider the person's ability only, not whether there is a position available to support this growth.)		

2. Could the employee perform at a higher level, in a different position, or take on increased responsibilities within the next three years? (Consider the person's ability only, not whether there is a position available to support this growth.)		
3. Can you envision this employee performing two levels above his or her current position in the next five to six years?		
4. Is the organization likely to value growth of the skills and competencies of this employee over the next several years?		
5. Could the employee learn the additional skills and competencies he or she needs to be able to perform at a higher or different level?		
6. Does the employee demonstrate leadership ability—by showing initiative and vision, delivering on promised results, communicating effectively, and taking appropriate risks?		
7. Does the employee demonstrate an ability to comfortably interact with people at a higher level or in different areas?		
8. Does the employee demonstrate comfort with a broader company perspective than his or her job currently requires?		
9. Does the employee demonstrate flexibility and motivation to move into a job that might be different from any that currently exist?		
10. Does the employee welcome opportunities for learning and development?		
TOTALS		

To evaluate this employee's **potential**, calculate the total number of "yes" responses and use the following scoring:
0–3 = Low; 4–7 = Medium; 8–10 = High

Use the number of "yes" answers from Parts I and II to determine the employee's placement on the grid below.

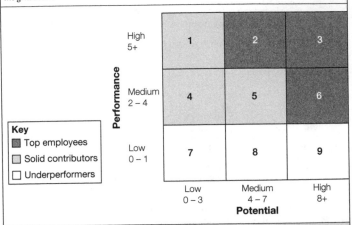

Key
- ■ Top employees
- ▨ Solid contributors
- ☐ Underperformers

Part IV: Strategies for Action

For employees in cells 2, 3, and 6 (top employees):

Use the following suggestions to create a development strategy.

Top Employees

- Recognize performance—Acknowledge the employee's achievements. Consider whether you are able to provide a special bonus, an opportunity to work on a special project, or some other form of reward. In the case of a person falling into cell 6, however, don't overly praise performance, because this person might be capable of achieving even more if properly motivated.
- Explore the employee's interests and values—What types of work excite him or her? What does he or she enjoy doing? Are there types of projects the employee hasn't worked on that he or she would like to try? What motivates the employee at work (e.g., challenging assignments, financial reward, public recognition, etc.)? Is he or she interested in taking on more responsibility? Are there outside constraints that might limit his or her ability to take on certain roles?
- Define the employee's skills—What is the employee good at? Are there any skill gaps (especially for employees in cell 6)? Are there skills you would like to see strengthened or developed?

- Explore creative opportunities for growth—Consider assignments that match the employee's interests and might help him or her learn new skills.
- Be honest about career possibilities within your organization—Is there a likely opportunity for advancement within your company? If not, what are other possible opportunities (e.g., working in a new area or leading a special project) for this employee in the long term?
- Create an individual development plan—Once your discussions are complete, outline suggested next steps and get agreement from the employee on the recommended course of action. Continue to follow up with and support your employee.

For employees in cells 1, 4, and 5 (solid performers):

Use the following suggestions to create a development strategy.

Solid Performers

- Focus on performance—Recognize and reward good work. These employees are of great value to the organization—let them know it. In the case of employees in cells 4 or 5, also clarify your expectations going forward. How might they be able to achieve even more?
- Explore the employee's interests and values—What types of work excite the employee? What does he or she enjoy doing? Are there types of projects the employee hasn't worked on that he or she would like to try? What motivates the employee at work (e.g., challenging assignments, financial reward, public recognition, etc.)? Is he or she interested in taking on more responsibility? Are there outside constraints that might limit his or her ability to take on certain roles? Test for evidence of more potential.
- Define the employee's skills—What are the employee's strengths? What skills does he or she need to further develop?
- Focus on motivating and engaging the employee in his or her work—What opportunities match this person's interests and development needs? If this person is interested in taking on more responsibility, how will you support his or her efforts? Perhaps look for special projects to test for motivation. In the case of someone in cell 4 or 5, watch for change in both performance and potential.
- Discuss career opportunities and limitations—Identify a possible career path. Don't make any promises at this point—just discuss the possibilities. Recognize any limitations in potential (e.g., is an advanced degree or supervisory experience required?). Be honest about the possibilities. If it is unlikely that the person will advance within the company, what other opportunities exist?
- Create an individual development plan—Once your discussions are complete, outline suggested next steps and get agreement from the employee on the recommended course of action. Continue to follow up with and support him or her.

For employees in cells 7, 8, and 9 (underperformers):
Use the following suggestions to create a development strategy.

Underperformers

- Focus on performance, not potential—Your conversation with individuals in this group should be about performance improvement, not about development. Provide honest feedback about performance. Explore the reasons why underperformers are not performing (Do they dislike this particular job's responsibilities? Do they feel like there is no opportunity for advancement? Are there personal issues that are affecting their work?).
- Clearly define your expectations for improvement—What changes will you be looking for? What are the consequences if the person does not improve? Work with your human resource department to develop a strategy for addressing poor performance.
- Define potential if performance is addressed—If the person has the potential to do more (i.e., is located in cells 8 and 9), consider what other opportunities might exist if the poor performance is addressed. Is this person in the wrong job?
- Create a performance improvement plan—Once your discussions are complete, outline suggested next steps and get agreement from the employee on the recommended course of action.

Manager's Planning Worksheet for Development Discussions

Use the following questions to help you think about your direct report's needs and goals before you conduct a development discussion. You may need to have a preliminary discussion with your employee to complete this form.

Employee Name:

Interests and Values

What are the employee's professional interests? What types of projects does he or she enjoy?

What do you perceive as being the employee's lifestyle needs based on what you have observed in the workplace? *For example, limited or no travel, set work schedule to meet outside responsibilities, etc.*

What do you think motivates this employee? *For example, compensation, high-visibility projects, public recognition, etc.*

Skills: Strengths and Gaps

What are the employee's top five skills?

What two or three skills does the employee need to learn in order to grow in his or her current job, advance to the next level, or seek a new job?

Performance and Potential

Is this employee currently performing up to his or her potential? If not, what do you think is preventing him or her from achieving better results?

Does this employee have an interest in taking on more responsibility?

Does this employee's performance record and potential support the possibility of taking on more responsibility? Explain.

Opportunities and Next Steps

Do opportunities exist within your group and/or the company for this employee to advance?

If so, what are they?

If not, what other opportunities are available to this employee? *For example, increased responsibilities, work in different subject area, etc.*

Individual Development Plan Worksheet

Use this form to help strengthen an employee's professional abilities by matching the individual's skills, business interests, and work values with opportunities for growth.

Developmental Goals	Measures of Achievement/Expected Outcomes
1.	
2.	
3.	

Methods to Be Used

On-the-Job Learning

What challenging assignments should this employee work on to build skills and achieve developmental goals? List the goal number next to each item.

Goal #	Type of Assignment	Time Frame

Training/Education

What specific training, educational experiences, and performance support measures (including online learning) can be used to develop desired skills and assist in achieving the employee's goals? List the goal number next to each item.

Goal #	Type of Training/Education/Support	When	Cost Estimate

Support Needed

What additional support is needed to achieve the employee's goals (e.g., coaching, mentoring, etc.)? How will it be provided?

Monitoring Progress

Who will provide feedback on the employee's progress, and how often? Be as specific as you can regarding who is involved and how often progress will be assessed.

Time Frame

Start date of plan: Anticipated completion date:

Agreement — This plan is agreed to as indicated by the signatures below.

Plan Participant	Date	Manager	Date

Test Yourself

This section offers ten multiple-choice questions to help you identify your baseline knowledge of the essentials of performance
appraisal.

Answers to the questions are given at the end of the test.

1. Why is it valuable to differentiate your employees in terms of
performance and potential?

   a. So you can identify which members of your team should be
developed, and which require performance improvement.

   b. So you can identify underachievers and dedicate more time
to helping them to reach their full potential.

   c. So you can identify top performers and focus all of your
development time on increasing their skills—and keeping
them happy.

2. What is the return-on-management ratio?

   a. A calculation to help you identify which employees are
underperforming.

   b. A framework for evaluating your strategic focus on daily
tasks.

   c. A metaphor for differentiating employees.

3. One of your direct reports has not been meeting performance goals for the past two weeks. You've already had a brief conversation with her about this, but she still hasn't improved. Now you are concerned that her poor work habits are bringing the rest of your group down. What should you do?

   a. Meet with her to prepare an individual development plan to identify projects that could help her improve her skills and her job satisfaction.

   b. Continue to document specific instances of her poor performance and watch to see if it continues for at least two more weeks.

   c. Meet with her to outline her performance expectations and establish a time frame for improvement.

4. Which of the following is *not* a good way to develop competent—but not exceptional—employees?

   a. Avoid giving them stretch opportunities because they are most likely content in their current position.

   b. Focus on coaching these employees to help them maximize their potential.

   c. Demonstrate your trust by allowing them to take actions and make decisions that are appropriate for their skill level.

5. Which of the following is a manager's role in developing employees?

   a. Taking responsibility for getting your top performers new positions if they want them.

b. Finding mentors for all of your solid performers.

c. Matching your solid and high performers' interests with opportunities.

6. Which of the following is or are intrinsic motivators?

a. Growth and learning opportunities.

b. Salary and other compensation forms.

c. Status within the organization.

7. Which of the following statements is true about a development discussion?

a. You'll prepare for each career development discussion in a similar way.

b. You should bring a completed individual development plan for your employee to your discussion.

c. You should start the discussion by sharing your perception of the employee's skills and interests.

8. With which category of employee would you most likely need to watch for signs of burnout?

a. Underperformers.

b. Solid contributors.

c. Top employees.

9. Which of the following is *not* a good reason to differentiate your employees?

a. To determine which of your employees are your favorites.

b. To identify which employees should be developed.

c. To decide the types of assignments to give each employee.

10. Which of the following is an example of a question used in the Performance and Potential Grid about an employee's *potential*?

a. Is the employee a key contributor to the team and the organization?

b. Does the employee regularly work overtime to complete challenging projects?

c. Could the employee learn the additional skills and competencies he or she needs to be able to perform at a higher or different level?

Answers to test questions

1, a. Differentiating employees helps you to identify who on the team should be developed—namely, your top and solid performers. Developing employees can be time-consuming, so you'll want to optimize the amount of time you spend on this activity. The return-on-management ratio suggests that you spend the *most* time working with the people who will contribute the most to your organization. Determining who your top and solid contributors are will help you focus your energy and time on them.

2, b. The return-on-management (ROM) ratio provides a way for managers to assess whether they are investing time and energy in activities that best contribute to their organization's productivity and overall performance. This ratio is useful for all management activities. In the case of developing employees, the ROM ratio suggests that managers spend the most time working with the people who contribute the most and add the most value to the organization.

3, c. Once you identify a poor performer, the first step is to try to move him or her up to an acceptable performance level. To do this, you'll want to provide clearly defined goals with specific timelines for achieving them. Sit down with the underperforming employee to discuss his or her performance issues. Be sure to let the employee know that you are willing to provide coaching and candid feedback to assist him or her in meeting performance expectations.

4, a. Although some solid contributors are not eager to advance within your organization, you shouldn't assume that they are all content in their current roles. The first step is to understand their interests, values, and skills. Find out what direction they'd like their career to take. Stretch assignments combined with coaching or mentoring may be exactly what some of these employees need to feel motivated to achieve greater results. Match employees to these assignments carefully, however, to ensure that you don't overwhelm them.

5, c. Effective employee development depends on your ability to match an individual's core interests, work values, and skills with appropriate growth opportunities. Ideally, these opportunities would map to organizational needs. Although you are responsible for guiding your employees, they must own the process of managing their careers.

6, a. Intrinsic motivation relies on factors that are related to job content. In addition to opportunities for growth and learning, intrinsic motivators include on-the-job achievement, positive feedback, and a sense of responsibility for the work an employee is doing.

7, a. Although the content of your career development conversations will differ depending on the employee and his or her performance and potential, you will prepare for each discussion in the same way. Start by gathering data to support the discussion. Then, clarify how ready you are to conduct the conversation by making sure you have a grasp of the employee's skills, interests, and values. Also, list potential opportunities that match these skills, interests, and values.

8, c. Although any employee can feel overwhelmed by his or her workload, top-performing employees are most often prone to overwork. In addition, managers are more likely to overload star performers than they are other employees—and many high achievers find it difficult to say "no" to more work. If you ask too much of your A players, you risk losing them. Watch for signs of burnout. And find ways to get more resources on a project or encourage a star performer to take a day off or a vacation.

9, a. Differentiation should *not* be a process by which you pass judgment on which employees are your favorites. Instead, it is a way to determine how to provide your direct reports with appropriate job and growth opportunities. Through differentiating, you identify those employees who can be targeted for development along with those who should instead focus on performance improvement.

10, c. This question addresses the employee's potential—his or her ability to learn the additional skills or competencies necessary to perform at a higher level in the future. In order to complete the Performance and Potential Grid, a manager must answer two sets of questions: one that assesses an employee's past results (performance), and the other that tries to predict the employee's ability to perform at a higher level in the future (potential). Using a tool that considers both an employee's performance and potential helps managers determine who their top, competent, and underperforming employees are. It also helps them decide on an appropriate course of action for each employee.

To Learn More

Articles

Axelrod, Helen Handfield-Jones, and Ed Michaels. "A New Game Plan for C Players." *Harvard Business Review* OnPoint Enhanced Edition. Boston: Harvard Business School Publishing, January 2002.

It's a big driver of business success, but one that executives are loath to talk about: upgrading the management talent pool by weeding out C players—those who deliver results that are acceptable but who fail to innovate or inspire the people they lead. This article explores the hidden costs of tolerating underperformance and acknowledges the reasons why executives may shy away from dealing decisively with C players. The authors outline steps for executives to take to execute a rigorous, disciplined process for assessing and dealing with low-performing managers while still treat them with respect.

Gary, Loren. "The Controversial Practice of Forced Ranking." *Harvard Management Update,* October 2001.

Bell-curve-based methods of identifying a company's worst-performing employees have become prevalent in performance management systems. The intentions—ratcheting up the quality and motivation of the workforce—are certainly laudable.

But in practice, does forced ranking cause more harm than good? And, is it the best means of improving the average quality of the workforce? Talent management experts offer the positives and negatives of forced ranking and the possible effects it can have in an organization.

Keller Johnson, Lauren. "Real Time Learning: How the Best Companies and Leaders Make It Happen." *Harvard Management Update,* January 2005.

When companies fail to develop their best people through experiential learning, they miss the chance to build up the bench strength required to stay ahead of rivals and ensure smooth succession as top leaders retire. Even the most talented executives and managers can't gain the skills they need to express their full potential. So how do the few succeed where the majority does not? They confront the obstacles to experiential learning and design effective processes to spur, support, and sustain leaders' professional growth. Learn how you, too, can capture the lessons of experiential learning.

Morison, Robert, Tamara Erickson, and Ken Dychtwald. "Managing Middlescence." *Harvard Business Review* OnPoint Enhanced Edition. Boston: Harvard Business Publishing, March 2006.

Today, millions of midcareer men and women are wrestling with middlescence—looking for ways to balance work, family, and leisure while hoping to find new meaning in their jobs. The question is: Will they find it in your organization or elsewhere? Companies are ill-prepared to manage middlescence because it is so pervasive, largely invisible, and culturally uncharted. That neglect is bad for business. Many companies risk losing some of their best people or—even worse—ending up with an army of disaffected people who stay. The best way to engage middlescents is to tap into their hunger for renewal and help them launch into more meaningful roles. Perhaps managers can't grant a promotion to everyone who merits one in today's flat organizations, but you may be able to offer new training, fresh assignments, mentoring opportunities, or even sabbaticals or entirely new career paths within your own company.

Rifkin, Glenn. "Building Better Global Managers." *Harvard Management Update,* March 2006.

Though strides have been made in developing successful global managers, it is a sad truth that too many companies assume that they can do things abroad in the same manner as they do them domestically. As a result, most managers still lack the necessary cultural awareness when dealing with overseas employees and partners, as well as the experience of managing increasingly complex processes long distance. Learn the steps leaders can take to develop in prospective global managers the empathic qualities necessary for working with individuals and systems that are unlike their own.

Simons, Robert L., and Antonio Davila. "How High Is Your Return on Management?" *Harvard Business Review* OnPoint Enhanced Edition. Boston: Harvard Business Publishing, April 2005.

Return on management (ROM) is a new ratio that gauges the payback from a company's scarcest resource: managers' time and energy. Unlike other business ratios, ROM is a rough estimate, not an exact percentage. It is also uniquely designed to reflect how well a company implements its strategy. Knowing which organizational factors conspire against or work to maximize an organization's productive energy will help managers calculate a rough measure for this equation. Harvard Business School Professor Robert Simons and HBS doctoral student Antonio Davila offer five "acid tests" to help managers measure their company's ROM.

Books

Knowdell, Richard L. *Building a Career Development Program*. Palo Alto: Davies-Black Publishing, 1996.

Drawing on his eighteen years of experience designing career development and train-the-trainer programs around the world, career counselor and organizational consultant Richard L. Knowdell offers a clear model of employee career management and provides the tools—guidelines, exercises, worksheets, and self-assessments—for implementing such a program in your organization. Describing concrete roles for top managers, human resource professionals, and employees, this book shows how to start a career development program that will benefit the entire organization and all those who take part.

Michaels, Ed, Helen Handfield-Jones, and Beth Axelrod. *The War for Talent*. Boston: Harvard Business School Press, 2001.

In 1998, a landmark *McKinsey Quarterly* article exposed the "war for talent" as a critical business challenge and a fundamental driver of corporate performance. Now, just when you thought it was over, the authors present compelling evidence that the war for talent will persist over the next two decades despite the twists and turns of the economy. In this definitive guide, the authors present a strategic view of what managers must do to win the war for talent. Drawing on their five years of research, including surveys of 13,000 executives and case studies of twenty-seven companies (including Amgen, GE, PerkinElmer, and The Home Depot), they map out five bold imperatives for attracting, developing, and retaining the very best people. Most important, they show that great talent management has more to do with a pervasive "talent mind-set" than it does with better HR processes.

Motivating People for Improved Performance: The Results-Driven Manager Series. Boston: Harvard Business School Press, 2005.

If talent is an organization's most important asset, maximizing that talent is its most critical challenge. This guide helps managers develop the skills to motivate people to perform at their best: make work meaningful and rewarding, foster commitment and innovation, and retain top performers.

Sources for Developing Employees

The following sources aided in development of this book:

Alvey, Susan. Interview on developing employees, Boston, July 2005.

Axelrod, Beth, Helen Handfield-Jones, and Ed Michaels. "A New Game Plan for C Players." *Harvard Business Review* OnPoint Enhanced Edition. Boston: Harvard Business School Publishing, January 2002.

Buckingham, Marcus, and Curt Coffman. *First, Break All the Rules: What the World's Greatest Managers Do Differently.* New York: Simon & Schuster, 1999.

DeLong, Thomas J., and Vineeta Vijayaraghavan. "Let's Hear It for B Players." *Harvard Business Review* OnPoint Enhanced Edition, June 2003.

Gary, Loren. "The Controversial Practice of Forced Ranking." *Harvard Management Update,* October 2001.

Gary, Loren. "Performance Management That Drives Results." *Harvard Management Update,* September 2004.

"Having the Career Development Discussion," Harvard Business School Publishing Training Program, September 2004.

Herzberg, Frederick. "One More Time: How Do You Motivate Employees?" *Harvard Business Review,* January 2003.

Keller Johnson, Lauren. "Real-Time Learning: How the Best Companies and Leaders Make It Happen." *Harvard Management Update,* January 2005.

Knowdell, Richard L. *Building a Career Development Program.* Palo Alto: Davies-Black Publishing, 1996.

McFarland, Jennifer. "Time to Get Serious About Talent Management." *Harvard Management Update,* June 2001.

Michaels, Ed, Helen Handfield-Jones, and Beth Axelrod. *The War for Talent.* Boston: Harvard Business School Press, 2001.

Motivating People for Improved Performance: The Results-Driven Manager Series. Boston: Harvard Business School Press, 2005.

Simons, Robert L., and Antonio Davila. "How High Is Your Return on Management?" *Harvard Business Review* OnPoint Enhanced Edition. Boston: Harvard Business School Publishing, April 2005.

Notes

Notes

Notes

Notes

Notes

Notes

Notes

How to Order

Harvard Business School Press publications are available world-wide from your local bookseller or online retailer.

You can also call:
1-800-668-6780

Our product consultants are available to help you 8:00 a.m.–6:00 p.m., Monday–Friday, Eastern Time. Outside the U.S. and Canada, call: 617-783-7450.

Please call about special discounts for quantities greater than ten.

You can order online at:
www.HBSPress.org